14
Scriptural Principles for Daily Living Vol. 2

14 Scriptural Principles for Daily Living Vol. 2

"Your words are a flashlight to light the path ahead of me and keep me from stumbling."
[Psalm 119:105 TLB]

Anthony Adefarakan

GLOEM, CANADA

CONTENTS

Dedication	1
Acknowledgement	2
Introduction	4
Principle #1 The Power of Applied Knowledge	7
Principle #2 Dealing with Borrowed Vessels	11
Principle #3 Remember Lot's Wife	15

CONTENTS

Principle #4 | By their Fruits - Not Works — 19

Principle #5 | Watch Your Mouth — 23

Principle #6 | The Peril of Inaction — 27

Principle #7 | Grace is not Lawlessness — 30

Principle #8 | Expecting His Unexpected Arrival — 33

Principle #9 | You are the Target — 37

Principle #10 | Promise is a Debt — 40

Principle #11 | Your Prayer – Your Benefit — 44

CONTENTS

Principle #12 | Fear Not 48

Principle #13 | The Spirit of Liberty 52

Principle #14 | It's Turning Again 55

| Conclusion 59

| WHY YOU REALLY NEED JESUS! 60

| PRAYER POINTS 65

| BECOME A FINANCIAL PARTNER WITH JESUS 66

| About the Author 69

Dedication

I dedicate this book to God Almighty for His goodness and faithfulness in making His Word available to me. All glory to His Holy Name.

Also to everyone desirous of a closer walk with God, living out His precepts on a daily basis, I am in agreement with you all and I decree that grace for a closer walk with God is coming upon you in Jesus' Name.

Acknowledgement

I sincerely acknowledge my Eternal Father, Who alone is the Source of all wisdom. He is the Author and Finisher of my faith and it is of His fullness that the contents of this book have been drawn.

Also, I want to profoundly appreciate my dear parents – Prince and Mrs. Timothy Adefarakan – for bringing me up in the way of the Lord and for instilling righteousness consciousness in me. The wonderful education foundation I was given, coupled with their constant encouragement has empowered me to reach heights that were once beyond my imagination.

My most special appreciation goes to my sweetheart, Abisolami; without her help and support, I would never have enjoyed the conducive atmosphere needed to publish this book. I appreciate your love, encouragement, and the support you give at all times. Thank you so much. I love you, my Baby!

And to all my mentors in Ministry, I appreciate you all. Your investments in my life are not in vain. May the Lord reward you all in Jesus' Name.

Introduction

Life on earth has been described as a form of pilgrimage with eternity as man's final destination.

1 Peter 2:11 TLB says:
"Dear brothers, you are only visitors here. Since your real home is in heaven, I beg you to keep away from the evil pleasures of this world; they are not for you, for they fight against your very souls."

And Hebrews 11:13 also says:
"These men of faith I have mentioned died without ever receiving all that God had promised them; but they saw it all awaiting them on ahead and were glad, for they agreed that this earth was not their real home but that they were just strangers visiting down here."

In the course of this brief earthly sojourn, we

are bound to face certain situations capable of generating questions like *'what step do I take?' 'where do I settle?' 'who do I marry?' 'will I be rich or poor?' 'how do I finance my projects?' 'how do I take good care of my family?' 'how do I know God's will for my life?'* just to mention a few. Usually, we find it difficult to provide correct answers to these questions due to our weak mortal nature.

However, there is a manual for this pilgrimage, which is the Word of God. The One Who designed this journey for us has put in the manual all we need to navigate our way successfully and to eventually end up on the glorious side of eternity when the pilgrimage is over. Little wonder David prayed in Psalm 119:19 – *"I am a stranger in the earth; hide not thy commandment from me".*

The principles presented in this Volume 2 are equally all Bible-based and will deliver results every time they are applied because the Word of God is forever settled in Heaven (Psalm 119:89).

I pray as you read on, God's grace to apply these principles will rest upon you in Jesus' Name.

Anthony Adefarakan.

Principle #1

The Power of Applied Knowledge

John 13:17 KJV says *"If ye know these things, happy are ye if ye do them."*

And James 1: 22-25 NLT says *"But don't just listen to God's word. You must do what it says. Otherwise, you are only fooling yourselves. For if you listen to the word and don't obey, it is like glancing at your face in a mirror. You see yourself, walk away, and forget what you look like. But if you look carefully into the perfect law that sets you free, and if you do what it says and don't forget what you heard, then God will bless you for doing it."*

Contrary to the popular saying that knowledge

is power; I put it to you that knowledge is not yet power until it is correctly applied. It's not really what you know that generates your desired results; rather, it is what you do with what you know that commands results.

What are you doing with what you know? Did you notice that John 13:17 quoted above says your happiness is only dependent on your doing and not on your knowing? There is no sense in acquiring information if you aren't going to do anything about it.

Look at what happened in the story of the woman with the issue of blood as recorded in Mark 5:25-34. She had heard about Jesus and she made a decision to get her healing simply by touching His garment. Verse 28 according to KJV says *"For she said, If I may touch His clothes, I shall be whole."* She knew touching the garment of Jesus would draw His healing power into her body. Now, that's knowledge. But even with this knowledge, her problem still remained. However, the moment she acted out what she knew (by actually touching the garment of Jesus), her 12 years old infirmity dried up right there. It was when this woman decided to do something about what she knew that her problem became solved. And according to John 13:17, that was when she became happy.

You know God answers prayers; there is no doubt about it in your heart. That's great! But until you pray, that knowledge will do you no good. You have to actually pray in order to receive and enjoy the answers to your prayers.

Also, you know that saving a portion of your income is good. You even know people who have been able to send their children to good schools because they saved towards it. You talk so much about it because it's such a smart thing to do. But did you know until you actually start saving a portion of your own income, that knowledge about savings will do you no good? You won't be able to do the things others who save are doing because you only know about saving, you don't do it.

According to James 1:22-25 quoted above, if

all you do is read or listen to God's Word without practicing what it says, you won't be blessed in all you do. Don't just read or listen to the Word; do what it says, and the blessedness of obedience will find its way into your life. The Bible says to give, pray, fast, forgive, judge not, help others, love others, etc. Do as it says and your life will enjoy beautiful blessings.

Remember, knowledge is not yet power until it is correctly applied.

Principle #2

Dealing with Borrowed Vessels

Matthew 16:21-23 KJV says *"From that time forth began Jesus to shew unto his disciples, how that he must go unto Jerusalem, and suffer many things of the elders and chief priests and scribes, and be killed, and be raised again the third day. Then Peter took him, and began to rebuke him, saying, Be it far from thee, Lord: this shall not be unto thee. But he turned, and said unto Peter, Get thee behind me, Satan: thou art an offence unto me: for thou savourest not the things that be of God, but those that be of men."*

Simon Peter had just got a divine revelation concerning the identity of Jesus Christ and he was commended for it (Matthew 16:13-19). However, shortly after that (in verses 21-23 quoted above), Jesus started talking to His disciples about his imminent suffering and death when Peter suddenly began to rebuke Him and telling Him none of those things would happen to Him. He was in other words telling Jesus that He would not suffer and He would not die (which happened to be His purpose for coming into the world in the first place). So technically, Peter was like telling Jesus that He would not fulfill His destiny.

Now, how did Jesus respond? He turned, looked at Peter, and said *'Get thee behind me, Satan...'*

Jesus was looking at Peter but He was addressing the devil. Why? Because He knew the devil had quickly borrowed Peter for a few minutes to frustrate His purpose of coming into the world. Notice Jesus looked into Peter's eyes but didn't blame him or fight him; rather He rebuked the devil in him.

The devil is a 'user'. He borrows unsuspecting human vessels to carry out his evil plans in other people's lives and in the world at large. He could borrow a husband and use him to frustrate his wife or even kill her. He could borrow children to become sources of nightmares to their parents. He could borrow employers and use them to make life so difficult for their employees. He could even borrow careless Pastors and direct them to preach misleading sermons to their congregations. The devil takes pleasure in using people to carry out his agenda so no one would suspect he is the one responsible. The vessel would be the one to suffer all the repercussions while he laughs and works on getting other borrowed vessels.

Your enemies are not the people working or speaking against you, they are only borrowed vessels.

Address the devil in them and they may turn out as your best friends. Think about that!

Jesus dealt with the devil speaking through the mouth of Peter and turned him into the Pillar of

His Church. All men are valuable to God; address the devil in them and see what beauty God can bring out of such lives.

Mary Magdalene was a very useful instrument during Jesus' earthly ministry. As a matter of fact, she was the first to see Jesus after His resurrection. But did you know that same Mary was previously possessed with seven demons? Read Mark 16:9. She was someone some cultures would call a terrible witch. How then did she become a major helper of ministry to Jesus? It's because Jesus dealt with the devil in her and brought out the best in her.

Also, it is worth mentioning that we must all be on the alert (through much watching and prayers) so that the devil will not turn us into one of his borrowed vessels. May the Lord frustrate all his plans against you and your family in Jesus' Name. Amen.

Principle #3

Remember Lot's Wife

Luke 17:32 KJV says *'Remember Lot's wife'*.

What happened to Lot's wife?

Let's look at Genesis 19:15-26 KJV.

"And when the morning arose, then the angels hastened Lot, saying, Arise, take thy wife, and thy two daughters, which are here; lest thou be consumed in the iniquity of the city. And while he lingered, the men laid hold upon his hand, and upon the hand of his wife, and upon the hand of his two daughters; the LORD being merciful unto him: and they brought him forth, and set him without the city. And it came to pass, when they had brought them forth abroad, that he said, Escape for thy life; look not behind thee, neither stay thou in all the plain; escape to the moun-

tain, lest thou be consumed. And Lot said unto them, Oh, not so, my Lord: Behold now, thy servant hath found grace in thy sight, and thou hast magnified thy mercy, which thou hast shewed unto me in saving my life; and I cannot escape to the mountain, lest some evil take me, and I die: Behold now, this city is near to flee unto, and it is a little one: Oh, let me escape thither, (is it not a little one?) and my soul shall live. And he said unto him, See, I have accepted thee concerning this thing also, that I will not overthrow this city, for the which thou hast spoken. Haste thee, escape thither; for I cannot do anything till thou become thither. Therefore the name of the city was called Zoar.

The sun was risen upon the earth when Lot entered into Zoar. Then the LORD rained upon Sodom and upon Gomorrah brimstone and fire from the LORD out of heaven; And he overthrew those cities, and all the plain, and all the inhabitants of the cities, and that which grew upon the ground. But his wife looked back from behind him, and she became a pillar of salt."

The Lord was going to destroy Sodom and Gomorrah because of their sins. But because of His relationship with Lot's uncle (Abraham), He dispatched some angels to rescue him and his family from there before the destruction. The angels helped Lot, his wife and his two daughters out of the location to be destroyed with an express instruction that they shouldn't look back.

While escaping, Lot's wife looked back and became a pillar of salt.

Now Jesus said in the text above *'Remember Lot's Wife'*.

What was He saying?

Jesus was saying in essence- until you are SAVED, you are not SAFE. And to be really SAVED, YOU MUST NOT LOOK BACK TO WHERE YOU ARE BEING RESCUED FROM, NO MATTER HOW STRONG THE TEMPTATION IS TO DO SO.

The moment you surrender your life to Christ, you become a new creature, and old things are supposed to pass away (2 Corinthians 5:17). If you used to fornicate or commit any kind of sin before you became saved, you are not expected to look back into indulging in such again. You are not even supposed to think about it any longer let alone going back to it. You must cut all ties with your sinful past.

Lot's wife became a pillar of salt just for looking back! Once you are in God's Kingdom, there is no looking back.

Principle #4

By their Fruits - Not Works

Matthew 7:15-20 KJV says *"Beware of false prophets, which come to you in sheep's clothing, but inwardly they are ravening wolves. Ye shall know them by their fruits. Do men gather grapes of thorns, or figs of thistles? Even so every good tree bringeth forth good fruit; but a corrupt tree bringeth forth evil fruit. A good tree cannot bring forth evil fruit, neither can a corrupt tree bring forth good fruit. Every tree that bringeth not forth good fruit is hewn down, and cast into the fire. Wherefore by their fruits ye shall know them."*

Recognizing false prophets and false teachers

is not difficult, Jesus said *'by their fruits you shall know them'*: not by their works.

Some of these false prophets and false teachers may preach astounding sermons, give convincing prophecies, hold great ecclesiastical positions, perform unusual miracles, wear gorgeous suits or even engage powerful grammatical constructions when ministering; all these are mere works. And Jesus never said by their works you shall know them, but by their fruits.

As a matter of fact, in verses 22-23 of that same Matthew 17 Jesus said *"Many will say to me in that day, Lord, Lord, have we not prophesied in thy name? and in thy name have cast out devils? and in thy name done many wonderful works? And then will I profess unto them, I never knew you: depart from me, ye that work iniquity."*

Jesus is not as impressed by your works as He is by your fruits. He wants you to bear fruits and that's His main reason for choosing and saving you. He said in John 15:16 NKJV *'You did not choose Me, but I chose you and appointed you that you should go and bear fruit, and that your fruit should remain, that whatever you ask the Father in My name He may give you.'*

The most important things God expects from your life are fruits. Works only come as secondary to Him. He wants to see these fruits in your life: fruits of praise, thanksgiving, righteousness, holiness, mercy, graciousness, patience as well as those listed in Galatians 5:22 (love, joy, peace, goodness, gentleness, longsuffering, meekness, faith and self-control).

These are of greater value to Him than your miracles and sermons.

Aside from the fact that you can recognize false prophets by their fruits, you too need to work on your fruits to be sure you are not heading in the same direction with them.

Anyone doing the works of Christ without the

character or nature of Christ is an Anti-Christ, regardless of the title they bear. Watch out!

Principle #5

Watch Your Mouth

James 1:19 NKJV says *"...my beloved brethren, let every man be swift to hear, slow to speak, slow to wrath."*

And Psalm 34:12-14 says *"What man is he that desireth life, and loveth many days, that he may see good? Keep thy tongue from evil, and thy lips from speaking guile. Depart from evil, and do good; seek peace, and pursue it."*

Your mouth must be well managed if your life will not be full of troubles. Proverbs 18:21 TLB says *'Those who love to talk will suffer the consequences. Men have died for saying the wrong thing!'*

Nobody can quote what you didn't say. Be swift to listen but slow to speak.

There is a vivid description of the tongue as well as the damage it is capable of doing if not properly tamed in James 3:2-12 TLB. It reads: *'If anyone can control his tongue, it proves that he has perfect control over himself in every other way. We can make a large horse turn around and go wherever we want by means of a small bit in his mouth. And a tiny rudder makes a huge ship turn wherever the pilot wants it to go, even though the winds are strong.*

So also the tongue is a small thing, but what enormous damage it can do. A great forest can be set on fire by one tiny spark. And the tongue is a flame of fire. It is full of wickedness, and poisons every part of the body. And the tongue is set on fire by hell itself and can turn our whole lives into a blazing flame of destruction and disaster.

Men have trained, or can train, every kind of animal or bird that lives and every kind of reptile and fish, but no human being can tame the tongue. It is always ready to pour out its deadly poison. Sometimes it praises our heavenly Father, and sometimes it breaks out into curses against men who are made like God. And so blessing and cursing come pouring out of the same mouth. Dear brothers, surely this is not right! Does a spring of water bubble out first with fresh water and then with bitter water? Can you pick olives from a fig tree, or figs from a grape vine? No, and you can't draw fresh water from a salty pool.'

The power of life and death lies in the tongue. As a matter of fact, the Bible has a lot to say when it comes to the use of our mouth because it has the power to even determine how we end up in eternity.

The devil cannot afflict you until you supply him with the needed information. Remember it was the information Eve gave to him in the Garden of Eden that he eventually used against her. Learn to shut your mouth sometimes. The Bible says there is a time to speak and there is a time to be silent. You need to discern these times for your mouth to not get you into trouble.

In Mark 11:23 Jesus said you shall have whatsoever you say. And according to Numbers 14:28, it is what the Lord hears you say that He will do unto you. Watch your mouth!

If you have issues in this area, you may need to pray as the Psalmist did in Psalm 141:3; *'Set a watch, O LORD, before my mouth; keep the door of my lips'.*

Principle #6

The Peril of Inaction

James 2:14-26 ESV says *"What good is it, my brothers, if someone says he has faith but does not have works? Can that faith save him? If a brother or sister is poorly clothed and lacking in daily food, and one of you says to them, "Go in peace, be warmed and filled," without giving them the things needed for the body, what good is that? So also faith by itself, if it does not have works, is dead.*

But someone will say, "You have faith and I have works." Show me your faith apart from your works, and I will show you my faith by my works. You believe that God is one; you do well. Even the demons believe—and shudder! Do you want to be shown, you foolish person, that faith apart from works is useless? Was not Abraham our father justified by works when he offered up his son Isaac on the altar? You see that faith was active along with his works, and faith was completed by his works; and the Scripture was fulfilled that says, "Abraham believed God, and it was counted to him as righteousness"—and he was called a friend of God. You see that a person is justified by works and not by faith alone. And in the same way was not also Rahab the prostitute justified by works when she received the messengers and sent them out by another way? For as the body apart from the spirit is dead, so also faith apart from works is dead."

Inaction has been defined by a dictionary as lack of action where some is expected or appropriate. It is the greatest killer of faith.

Believing has never been so much of a problem for so many people. Rather, the problem has always been 'acting' out what is believed. What you believe can only be seen through your actions. How can you claim to believe *'you shall be the head and not the tail'* when everywhere you go, all you do is talk about how hard things are and even beg people for money? You really don't believe that.

Faith means "Stepping into what you believe God can do" and not just confessing it. Remember, River Jordan didn't part for the Israelites until the Levites stepped into it.

As the body without the spirit is dead, so is faith without a corresponding action. SAY AND ACT OUT WHAT YOU BELIEVE, THEREIN LIES YOUR TESTIMONY!

Principle #7

Grace is not Lawlessness

Romans 6:1-2 KJV says *"What shall we say then? Shall we continue in sin, that grace may abound? God forbid. How shall we, that are dead to sin, live any longer therein?"*

Grace, which has been popularly defined as unmerited favour, is not a license to go on sinning. It doesn't exempt you from being law-abiding, rather it empowers you to live above lawlessness.

Under the Old Covenant, certain laws were put in place to ensure people's compliance with God's demands. And breaking any of those laws attracted serious penalties.

For instance, in Exodus 31:12-17, the Lord had commanded the children of Israel that they must not do any work on the Sabbath day. He further warned that whoever broke that law would be put to death.

Now, something happened in Numbers 15:32-36 KJV;

'And while the children of Israel were in the wilderness, they found a man that gathered sticks upon the Sabbath day. And they that found him gathering sticks brought him unto Moses and Aaron, and unto all the congregation. And they put him in ward, because it was not declared what should be done to him. And the LORD said unto Moses, The man shall be surely put to death: all the congregation shall stone him with stones without the camp. And all the congregation brought him without the camp, and stoned him with stones, and he died; as the LORD commanded Moses.'

Did you see that? A man broke the law of the Sabbath and he paid with his life.

But now we are under grace; some of us even go to work on days of worship and we don't get stoned. Does that mean God no longer cares whether we worship Him or not? Or does that mean we no longer have to observe scheduled rest since we are no more under the law? Not at all. As a matter of fact, we do more under grace. We don't just worship God on certain days, we live a life of worship on daily basis. So just because there are no stones coming at us for not worshiping God or obeying His commands doesn't mean we now have the license to live as we please. Grace is not a license to sin; it's a divine enablement to overcome sin and even do beyond the requirements of the law.

Don't take God's grace for granted!

Principle #8

Expecting His Unexpected Arrival

Matthew 24:36-44 KJV says *"But of that day and hour knoweth no man, no, not the angels of heaven, but my Father only. But as the days of Noe were, so shall also the coming of the Son of man be. For as in the days that were before the flood they were eating and drinking, marrying and giving in marriage, until the day that Noe entered into the ark, And knew not until the flood came, and took them all away; so shall also the coming of the Son of man be. Then shall two be in the field; the one shall be taken, and the other left. Two women shall be grinding at the mill; the one shall be taken, and the other left.*

Watch therefore: for ye know not what hour your Lord doth come. But know this, that if the goodman of the house had known in what watch the thief would come, he would have watched, and would not have suffered his house to be broken up. Therefore be ye also ready: for in such an hour as ye think not the Son of man cometh."

Had it been Jesus Christ came for His bride (the Church) today, would you have gone with Him? Well, if you aren't sure, thank God He didn't.

Jesus Christ ascended from this earth leaving us a promise of His return. He said He would come back for His saints when He is done preparing a place for us (John 14:1-3).

The early disciples tried to get Him to tell them when His return would be. And He told them point-blank that no one knows, not even the angels of heaven. He said only His Father knows the day and hour.

However, He gave them an idea that is equally relevant to us today. He said in verse 37 of Matthew 24 *'But as the days of Noah were, so shall also the coming of the Son of man be.'*

Now that's a clue. So the next thing would be to find out what happened in the days of Noah before the flood that destroyed the first world came.

Matthew 24:38 says they were eating and drinking; marrying and giving in marriage. Everything was going on fine; everyone was going about their normal activities until Noah entered the Ark and suddenly the flood came and destroyed them all.

As it was then, so also shall it be when He comes back to rapture His Church. Don't be carried away with parties, celebrations, career development, family affairs, and even ministerial activities. You must be ready at all times. In verse 44 of this same text, Jesus said *'Therefore be ye also ready: for in such an hour as ye think not the Son of man cometh.'*

Watch and Pray, the coming of the Lord doesn't respect days of ceremonies! Be sensitive.

Principle #9

You are the Target

1 Peter 5:8 KJV says *"Be sober, be vigilant; because your adversary the devil, as a roaring lion, walketh about, seeking whom he may devour:"*

If you are really a Christian, then you are always the devil's target. He hates your Master and seeks to deal with you for choosing to follow Him.

His plans against you include stealing, killing and destroying everything precious to you (John 10:10). Therefore, it's either you stop his assaults or he rubbishes your salvation testimony.

Now, with this consciousness of the plans of the devil (your great adversary), what attitude should it birth in you as a believer?

Let's read Ephesians 6:10-18 KJV:

'Finally, my brethren, be strong in the Lord, and in the power of his might. Put on the whole armour of God, that ye may be able to stand against the wiles of the devil. For we wrestle not against flesh and blood, but against principalities, against powers, against the rulers of the darkness of this world, against spiritual wickedness in high places. Wherefore take unto you the whole armour of God, that ye may be able to withstand in the evil day, and having done all, to stand. Stand therefore, having your loins girt about with truth, and having on the breastplate of righteousness; And your feet shod with the preparation of the gospel of peace; Above all, taking the shield of faith, wherewith ye shall be able to quench all the fiery darts of the wicked. And take the helmet of salvation, and the sword of the Spirit, which is the word of God:

Praying always with all prayer and supplication in the Spirit, and watching thereunto with all perseverance and supplication for all saints;'

Your attitude should be as described in those verses of Ephesians 6. You need to wear the full armour of God constantly without taking them off at any point in time.

Your helmet of salvation for instance must always be on your head because you don't know if your head is being aimed at. Wear your armour to bed; go out with it and return with it.

Remember the devil is still seeking whom he may devour; that will not be you or any member of your family in Jesus' Name.

Sign up for Jesus full time, grab your armour, and be on the alert. There is no middle ground!

Principle #10

Promise is a Debt

Proverbs 25:14 GNT says *"People who promise things that they never give are like clouds and wind that bring no rain."*

There are two dimensions to this subject of Promise. One is towards God while the other is towards man.

We will consider promises made to God first. You see, God is not looking for those who can impress Him. He is the Almighty God and there is nothing you can do to make Him love you more. The Bible says He has loved you with an everlasting love (Jeremiah 31:3). That is a perfect kind of love that doesn't depend on what you've done but on Who He is.

So, you don't have to make any promises to Him to get His attention. But if you must do, then you've got to make sure you fulfill it because to make promises (vows) to God and not keep it attracts His anger. Promise becomes a debt when you fail to keep it. If you won't keep it, don't promise it.

Look at what Ecclesiastes 5:2-6 GNT says;

'Think before you speak, and don't make any rash promises to God. He is in heaven and you are on earth, so don't say any more than you have to. The more you worry, the more likely you are to have bad dreams, and the more you talk, the more likely you are to say something foolish. So when you make a promise to God, keep it as quickly as possible. He has no use for a fool. Do what you promise to do. Better not to promise at all than to make a promise and not keep it. Don't let your own words lead you into sin, so that you have to tell God's priest that you didn't mean it. Why make God angry with you? Why let him destroy what you have worked for?'

That's what happens when you make promises to God and fail to keep them. It attracts some levels of destruction. Psalm 15:4 says even if the fulfillment of your promise to God hurts you, don't fail to keep it. Your integrity pleases Him. That's what happened to Jephthah in Judges 11:29-40. He made an impulsive vow to God and the fulfillment cost Him his only daughter. He didn't hold back. He gave her up. That's the kind of integrity God expects from you.

Now to the second dimension – promises made to man. God's Word says *'Owe no man...'* and that includes fulfilling your promises.

When you make promises and you fail to keep them, you are like a cloud that brings no rain. You raise people's expectations and you cause their eyes to fail while vainly expecting the fulfillment of your promises and that doesn't please God in any way. It's better to give what you have at the moment than to promise what you don't have and keep the other person waiting.

Politicians and lovers, please take note. Don't make promises or pledges you know you can't or won't keep. That will make you a debtor and your integrity will remain questionable regardless of what else you do right.

If you won't do it, don't promise it. A simple rule of life!

Principle #11

Your Prayer – Your Benefit

John 16:24 NIV says *"Until now you have not asked for anything in my name. Ask and you will receive, and your joy will be complete."*

Prayer doesn't change God, it changes you and positions you for all God wants you to have. You don't do God any favor by praying, you are the Principal beneficiary of your own prayers.

For instance, when Jabez prayed in 1 Chronicles 4:9-10, God's condition didn't improve; it was his own situation that got better.

He prayed *"'Oh that you would bless me and en-*

large my territory! Let your hand be with me, and keep me from harm so that I will be free from pain." And God granted his request.'

If you possess this *'I am the one benefitting'* attitude towards prayer, you will never need anyone to encourage you to pray anymore.

So stop complaining and start praying. God is waiting to hear your voice. The Bible says in Proverbs 15:8, 29 that God delights in the prayers of the upright and that He hears the prayers of the righteous. Your prayer is God's delight while your lamentation, grumbling, murmuring, and complaining are His nightmare. Give God daily delight by praying on a daily basis, and you will see the benefits of prayer constantly flowing into your life.

As I end this section, I will like to show you what complaining and murmuring can attract to you.

Look at Numbers 14:1-4; after some of the men who went to spy the Promised Land brought back a negative report that they couldn't possess the land because of the giants there, the children of Israel cried and murmured – *"And all the congregation lifted up their voice, and cried; and the people wept that night. And all the children of Israel murmured against Moses and against Aaron: and the whole congregation said unto them, Would God that we had died in the land of Egypt! or would God we had died in this wilderness! And wherefore hath the LORD brought us unto this land, to fall by the sword, that our wives and our children should be a prey? were it not better for us to return into Egypt? And they said one to another, Let us make a captain, and let us return into Egypt."*

They literally blamed God for rescuing them from their oppressors in Egypt and actually said they were better off there. God wasn't pleased with what they said and because those spies had said they looked like grasshoppers in the sight of the giants in that land and in their own eyes as well, the Lord made sure they died in the wilderness like grasshoppers (Numbers 14:26-37). Their carcasses fell in the wilderness as He promised. Only Joshua and Caleb together with those less than 20 years of age made it to the Promised Land. All those who murmured died.

Learn to pray about everything; don't be caught in the destructive web of murmuring and complaining.

Principle #12

Fear Not

Isaiah 41:10-13 NKJV says *"Fear not, for I am with you; Be not dismayed, for I am your God. I will strengthen you, Yes, I will help you, I will uphold you with My righteous right hand.'*

"Behold, all those who were incensed against you Shall be ashamed and disgraced; They shall be as nothing, And those who strive with you shall perish. You shall seek them and not find them—Those who contended with you. Those who war against you Shall be as nothing, As a nonexistent thing. For I, the Lord your God, will hold your right hand, Saying to you, 'Fear not, I will help you.'"

"Fear Not" as declared in the scriptures is not

just a form of encouragement, it is actually a command. When you are in fear, you are not in faith; and whatsoever is not of faith is SIN (Romans 14:23b).

Therefore, do not focus on your fears; rather expose them to THE FAITH-GENERATING WORD OF GOD (Romans 10:17), and they will simply disappear.

There is something in Deuteronomy 20:1-4 NKJV; it's one of the things to do when confronted with fearful situations. It reads: *"When you go out to battle against your enemies, and see horses and chariots and people more numerous than you, do not be afraid of them; for the Lord your God is with you, who brought you up from the land of Egypt. So it shall be, when you are on the verge of battle, that the priest shall approach and speak to the people. And he shall say to them, 'Hear, O Israel: Today you are on the verge of battle with your enemies. Do not let your heart faint, do not be afraid, and do not tremble or be terrified because of them; for the Lord your God is He who goes with you, to fight for you against your enemies, to save you.'*

The scripture quoted above has to do with warfare, and it might interest you to know that life itself is a battlefield.

Look at how you are to handle your moments of fear in that scripture even though you are looking at 'chariots, horses, and people more numerous than you'. It says you shouldn't be afraid because the God Who delivered you in times past is still with you and He is going to do it again.

So, you used to have a very terrible headache; you prayed to God and He healed you. Now years have passed and suddenly you got diagnosed with diabetes. They told you what can happen to you if it is not properly managed and fear suddenly gripped you. In this present condition, the Lord wants you to remember how He healed you when you had that terrible headache and He wants you to trust Him to handle this diabetes as well. Your faith is what moves God, not your fear.

Remembering God's past acts of deliverance is what gives you the courage to expect Him to handle the problems at hand.

Psalm 56:3 KJV says *'What time I am afraid, I will trust in thee'*. That should be your decision too.

Principle #13

The Spirit of Liberty

2 Corinthians 3:17 KJV says *"Now the Lord is that Spirit: and where the Spirit of the Lord is, there is liberty."*

With Jesus in your life, you are legally licensed to enjoy liberty from sin, shame, reproach, barrenness, limitation, sorrow, poverty among other negative circumstances of life. When you embrace Jesus, you embrace freedom!

The Ministry of Jesus Christ was summarized in Isaiah 61:1-3 KJV:
"The Spirit of the Lord God is upon Me,
Because the Lord has anointed Me
To preach good tidings to the poor;
He has sent Me to heal the brokenhearted,

To proclaim liberty to the captives,
And the opening of the prison
To those who are bound;
To proclaim the acceptable year of the Lord,
And the day of vengeance of our God;
To comfort all who mourn,
To console those who mourn in Zion,
To give them beauty for ashes,
The oil of joy for mourning,
The garment of praise for the spirit of heaviness;
That they may be called trees of righteousness,
The planting of the Lord,
That He may be glorified."

To those who are in darkness, the freedom they need is light and Jesus is the Light of the world. To those who are sick, the freedom they need is healing and Jesus is the Healer.

To those who are bound, the freedom they need is deliverance and Jesus is the Deliverer. There is nothing that sets free beyond the truth and Jesus happens to be the Way, the Truth, and the Life (John 14:6).

Get this from me today; accepting the Lordship of Jesus Christ over your life isn't just about securing your eternity in Heaven, it also guarantees a life of absolute freedom and dominion down here. You will never be able to know what freedom truly means until you totally surrender to Jesus Christ - Who alone is the Spirit of Liberty.

Principle #14

It's Turning Again

Psalm 126:1-3 KJV says *"When the LORD turned again the captivity of Zion, we were like them that dream. Then was our mouth filled with laughter, and our tongue with singing: then said they among the heathen, The LORD hath done great things for them. The LORD hath done great things for us; whereof we are glad."*

There is nothing pleasurable about captivity. It connotes confinement, incapacitation, and forced restriction. A person in captivity may have his own dreams but he is not at liberty to pursue them. Rather, they live to fulfill the dreams of their captors.

Any form of sickness or disease that prevents

you from living your life the way you normally would is a form of captivity. Anything at all that is preventing you from expressing your God-given potentials towards reaching your goal represents captivity. But here is the good news, the Lord Who turned the captivity of Zion is turning yours too. How am I so sure? Well, Hebrews 13: 8 says He is the same yesterday, today, and forever. That means what he did yesterday, He can and will do again today.

There are many stories in the Bible to prove to you that God actually turns people's captivities. But I will share just two with you in this chapter.

The first one is in John 5:2-9 KJV: *"Now there is at Jerusalem by the sheep market a pool, which is called in the Hebrew tongue Bethesda, having five porches. In these lay a great multitude of impotent folk, of blind, halt, withered, waiting for the moving of the water. For an angel went down at a certain season into the pool, and troubled the water: whosoever then first after the troubling of the water stepped in was made whole of whatsoever disease he had.*

And a certain man was there, which had an infirmity thirty and eight years. When Jesus saw him lie, and knew that he had been now a long time in that case, he saith unto him, Wilt thou be made whole? The impotent man answered him, Sir, I have no man, when the water is troubled, to put me into the pool: but while I am coming, another steppeth down before me. Jesus saith unto him, Rise, take up thy bed, and walk. And immediately the man was made whole, and took up his bed, and walked: and on the same day was the sabbath."

This man had been battling with an infirmity that kept him in one spot for 38 years. Now that is real captivity. All his dreams, aspirations, and plans were put on hold as a result of his infirmity. But when Jesus arrived on the scene, He turned his captivity and gave him a new beginning. He gave him the opportunity to become what he never dreamt he could become.

The second story is that of the mad man of Gadara according to Mark 5:1-20. This man was so mad that no one could bind him with chains, he would just tear them into pieces. In fact, he was literally living among the dead (in tombs). Now, without any form of doubt, that looked like a concluded case. Hopeless!

But Jesus didn't think so. He commanded the legion of demons (about 6,000) that had held this man captive to leave his body and set him completely free. He was so transformed that he became an evangelist in Decapolis (telling people about the One Who turned his captivity) and all the people marveled.

"When the Lord turned again the captivity of Zion, we were like them that dream". Honestly, I don't know how El-Adonai will do it, but before the end of this very year, you shall be congratulated. If you believe this, the first congratulation locates you within the next 24hours in the Name of Jesus. It is SETTLED!

Conclusion

So far, the Lord has revealed some biblical principles to us. The purpose is not just to know, document, or preach them, rather they were revealed so that we can walk in them.

According to John 8:32, only the truth that is known sets free. So, go through these principles one by one and determine to build your Christian walk around them for a life of Kingdom impact here on earth.

Jesus said in John 13:17(NLT) - *"You know these things- now do them! That is the path of blessing."*

May the Lord release upon you and your entire household the grace to walk worthy of His calling upon your lives in Jesus' Name!

WHY YOU REALLY NEED JESUS!

You might have heard a lot of Preachers talk about the importance of surrendering one's life to Jesus and even the dangers of not doing so at one time or the other without you being really moved. But with these three (3) important reasons highlighted below, I strongly believe you will not need another sermon before deciding to yield to His saving grace regardless of your religious beliefs.

1. **You have an Enemy to overcome:** There is an adversary who is all out to steal from you, kill you and destroy you regardless of your level of education, moral uprightness, societal influence, or even religious beliefs. He is Devil by name (John 10:10, 1 Peter 5: 8), and he doesn't release any of

his captives until he completely destroys their souls in hell. The ONLY One Who can deliver you from his manipulations and also save your soul from him is Jesus Christ.

2. **You have an Appointment to keep:** Being alive and reading this implies you have a very important and inevitable appointment to keep. It is an appointment with death (Hebrews 9:27). Death is the sure end of all mortals (of which you are part), and to enable you to prepare for this appointment without fear of eternal damnation, you need Jesus. He is the ONLY One Who has power over death (Revelation 1:18).

3. **You have a Judge to face:** Upon departure from this earth, you will have to stand before a judgment throne to render an account of your earthly life (Hebrews 9:27, Romans 14:12). The outcome of this judgment is what will determine your eternal abode which will either be Heaven

or the Lake of fire. Interestingly, the Judge Who will preside over your case and also decide where you will spend your eternity is Jesus (John 5:21-30, 2 Timothy 4:1). I perceive you are thinking "is God not our Judge? Why Jesus?' Well, you are not wrong. But God the Father Himself is the One Who handed over all the judgment to His Son, Jesus Christ. Read verse 22 of that John chapter 5. So Jesus is the ONLY One Who has the power to either judge you guilty or guiltless in eternity.

Now that you know these, the wisest thing you can do for yourself is to quickly establish a relationship with Jesus, since you don't even know how close your appointment with death is. To do this, say this prayer aloud:

"Lord Jesus, I am a sinner and I cannot help myself. Wash me in your precious blood and make me a new creature. I open the door of my heart to you today, come into my life, and become my Lord and Savior. Grant me the grace

to overcome the devil, prepare me for eternity, and help me to escape the judgment reserved for sinners. Thank You Jesus for saving me. Amen."

Congratulations! You are now SAVED. Go and sin no more.

To learn more about your new relationship with Jesus, kindly send an Email to info@gloem.org or emancipation4souls@yahoo.com, we will send you material that will help you. You can also call, text, or send a WhatsApp message to +1 587 9735910 or +1 587 9695910 for further assistance.

And to learn more about God, His Word, and His plans for your life, kindly visit our Facebook page [***https://www.facebook.com/gloem.org***] for daily meditation in the Word of God (all year round) and our Blog page [***https://gloem.org/my-blog***] for life-transforming publications.

You are also invited to listen to Freedom Podcast: The Official Weekly Podcast of Global Emancipation Ministries – Calgary via https://anchor.fm/gloem

All these great resources capable of developing your spiritual stamina will help you become an overcomer in life regardless of what comes your way.

PRAYER POINTS

1. Father, thank You for opening my eyes to the truths contained in this book.
2. Father, please cause every experience in my life to work together for my good.
3. I cancel everything contrary to my prosperity and advancement in Jesus' Name.
4. God of all possibilities, please cause my grass to become green again.
5. From today, my breakthrough shall no longer be delayed in Jesus' Name.
6. Father, beginning from now, please release upon me and my household the ability to walk with you faithfully in the Name of Jesus.
7. Father, I thank You for answering all my prayers. Glory be to Your Holy Name. Hallelujah!

BECOME A FINANCIAL PARTNER WITH JESUS

At *Global Emancipation Ministries - Calgary*, our mandate is *to liberate men through the knowledge of the Truth* and our mission statement is *creating channels through which men can encounter the Truth - [Isaiah 61:1-3; John 8:32, 36; I Thessalonians 5:24]*.

Our Ministerial Activities include Rural and Urban Evangelical Outreaches, Prison Evangelism, Hospital Ministrations, Mobilization for Missions Support, Teaching of the undiluted Word of God, Scripture-Based Seminars, Discipleship, Training of Field Missionaries and Empowerment of underprivileged ones among other Field Ministerial Tasks.

If you sense the Lord is calling you to reach out to the lost by engaging in any of these activities or by assisting those involved with your resources, please feel free to join us. Let us come together as we take the Gospel of our Lord Jesus Christ to the hurting and forgotten ones. [Mark 16:15-20].

Please join us in these kingdom projects by making your weekly, monthly, quarterly, or annual donations to Global Emancipation Ministries – Calgary.

You can visit the "GIVE" section on our website, www.gloem.org, to learn about the ways to give.

For acknowledgment, please advise your donations to us by email: info@gloem.org or emancipation4souls@yahoo.com, and kindly include your details i.e. name, address, email, and location. Alternatively, you can simply call +1 587 9735910 to do the same.

You can also volunteer your gifts and talents in the service of the Lord through our ministerial platforms regardless of your location. To get information on how to go about this, please visit www.gloem.org and contact us via email: info@gloem.org or emancipation4souls@yahoo.com.

God bless you.

About the Author

By the special grace of God, **Anthony O. Adefarakan** is the privileged President of **Global Emancipation Ministries - Calgary (GLOEM)** with headquarters in Canada, North America, and **Emancipating Truth Ministry International (ETMI)** with headquarters in Nigeria, West Africa.

The Lord called him into the field ministry in February 2008 with the mandate to liberate men through the knowledge of the Truth, and by December 2012 he was ordained and commissioned as the Pioneer Pastor – in – Charge of The Redeemed Christian Church of God, Revelation Parish, Shalom Area under Delta Province III, Nigeria where he served until 1st February 2015 when he officially handed over to a new Pastor in order to focus on his field ministry to which the Lord had earlier called him and for which the authority of the church had already prayed and released him to undertake.

On 29th September 2013, he was awarded a Post Graduate Diploma in Tent – Making Mission from the Redeemed Christian School of Missions, Nigeria (RECSOM, Asaba Campus) where he also had the privilege to train Pastors and Missionaries as a lecturer in 2017.

Since the commissioning of his field ministry in 2015 he has had the opportunity to lead his ministry officers to field ministrations in different Prisons, Hospitals, Orphanages, Rural communities, Camp settlements, Markets, Local churches among other places with great successes on all occasions – such as the salvation of sinners, healing of the sick, financial empowerment of mission churches, provision of relief materials to the poor, provision of medical services to the underprivileged, baptism in the Holy Ghost, deliverance from demonic oppression, the release of inmates just to mention a few - all to the glory of God Who alone is the Doer.

He is the author of other best-selling titles such as *The Law of Kinds, Learning From the Ants, The Immutability of God's Counsel, Surely there is an End, Life Applicable lessons from the Book of Ruth, One thing is Needful Weekly Devotional Guide, Life Applicable Revelations from God's Word* (Volumes 1 and 2) among others.

He is blissfully married to Ifeoluwa A. Adefarakan and their marriage is fruitful to the glory of God.

Jesus is his Message, Freedom is the Outcome!
Isaiah 61:1-3

ANTHONY ADEFARAKAN

www.ingramcontent.com/pod-product-compliance
Lightning Source LLC
Chambersburg PA
CBHW021430070526
44577CB00001B/150